Where Are We?

by Michelle Schaub

Table of Contents

I need to know these words.

buildings

map

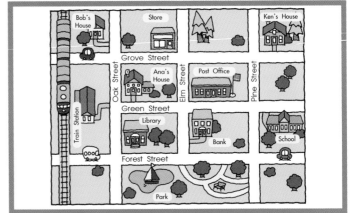

route

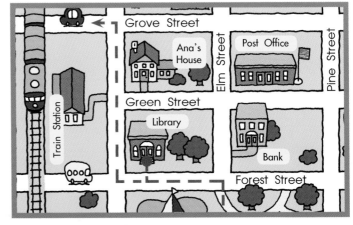

2

states

streets

town

3

What Is a Map?

A map is a drawing of an area.
A map has pictures of streets, buildings,
and other places.

▲ This picture shows
a town. Someone
took this picture
from an airplane.

▲ This map shows a town.

You can find a map of almost
any place.

▲ Maps can show states.

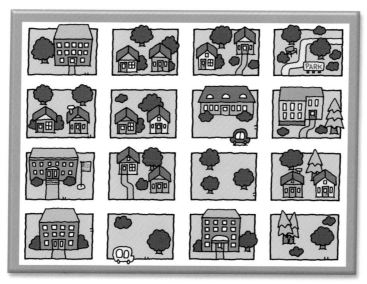

▲ Maps can show towns.

You can use a map to go almost anywhere. First, you need a place to begin. Next, find where you will end.

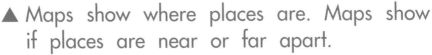
▲ Maps show where places are. Maps show if places are near or far apart.

Then use the map to plan your route.
Will you go straight ahead?
Will you turn left or right? A map
helps you find your way.

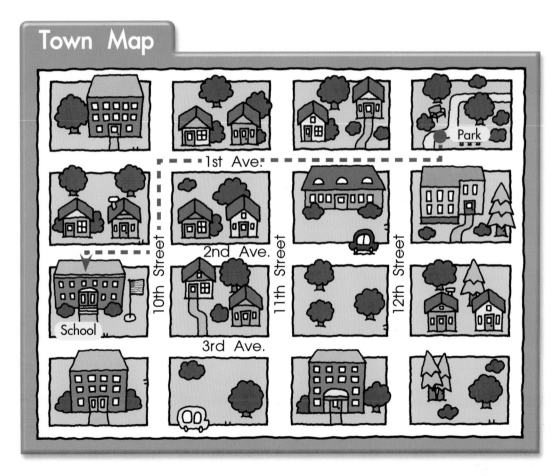

▲ This map shows how to go from the park
to the school.

How Do Maps Help Us?

Ken just moved to Hillside. How can Ken find his way around?

▲ Hillside is a small town.

Ken can use a map!
This map of Hillside will help Ken.

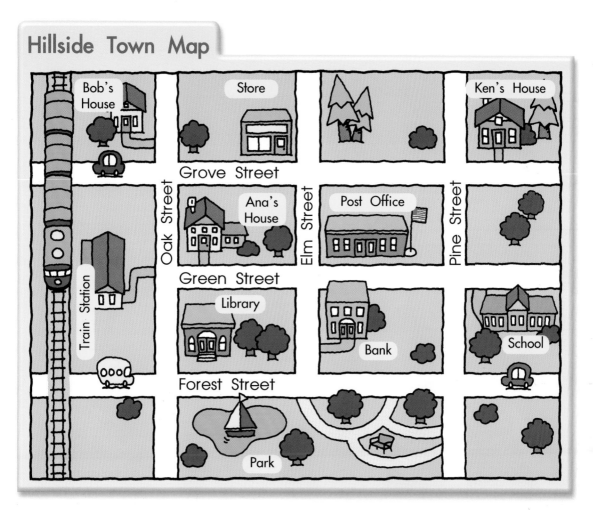

Hillside Town Map

Bob's House · Store · Ken's House · Grove Street · Oak Street · Ana's House · Elm Street · Post Office · Pine Street · Green Street · Train Station · Library · Bank · School · Forest Street · Park

▲ Look at the map. Where is Ken's house on the map?

Bob is in the park. Bob has two places to go. First, he wants to go to the library. Then Bob wants to go home. How will he get to these places?

▲ How can Bob get to the library and then home?

Bob starts at the park. Bob turns left on Forest Street. Bob goes into the library and returns a book. Then he turns right on Oak Street. He goes straight to his house.

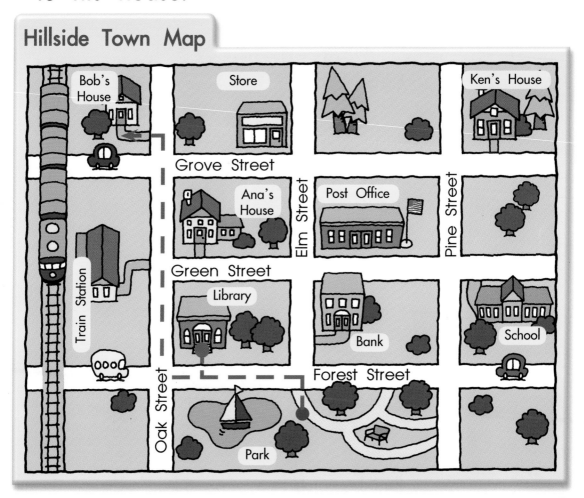

Hillside Town Map

▲ Follow Bob's route with your finger.

Can You Use a Map?

Ana must go to the store.
Ana must buy milk. How
will Ana get there?

▲ How can Ana get to
the store?

Ana is at her house. Find two ways that Ana can walk to the store.

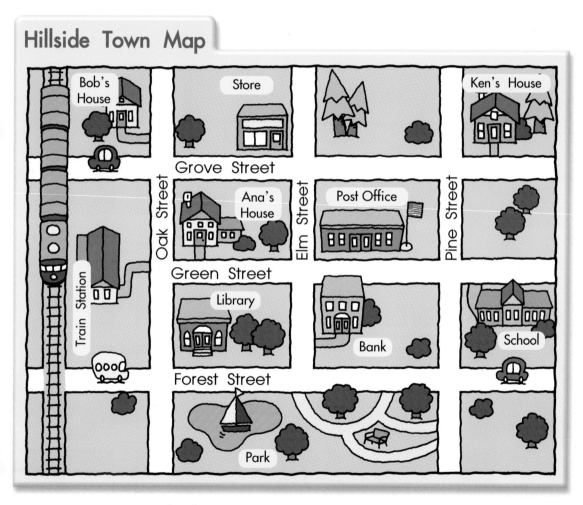

Hillside Town Map

Bob's House

Store

Ken's House

Grove Street

Oak Street

Ana's House

Elm Street

Post Office

Pine Street

Train Station

Green Street

Library

Bank

School

Forest Street

Park

▲ Which way can Ana go?

Tim wants to take his dog to the park. Can you find a way for Tim to go?

Tim's Route

Tim's House

Hospital

Main Street

Restaurant

Meadow Lane

Elm Street

Pine Street

Park

Cottage Place

▲ What is the shortest route for Tim to take?

Kate wants to go to Jen's house.
How will Kate get there?

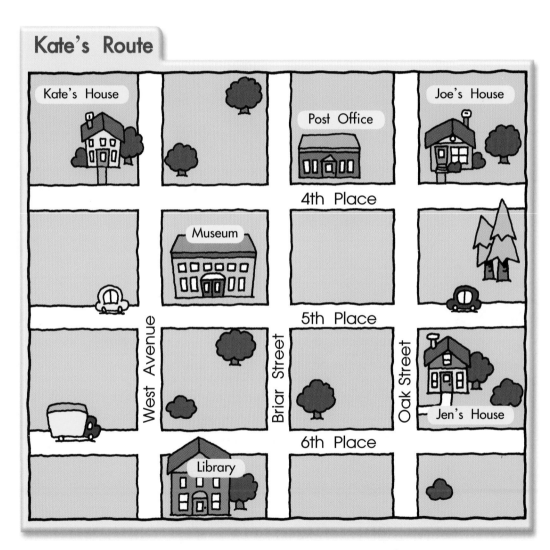

Kate's Route

Kate's House
Post Office
Joe's House
4th Place
Museum
5th Place
West Avenue
Briar Street
Oak Street
Jen's House
6th Place
Library

▲ Trace Kate's route with your finger.

Now you can use a map. Where will you go?